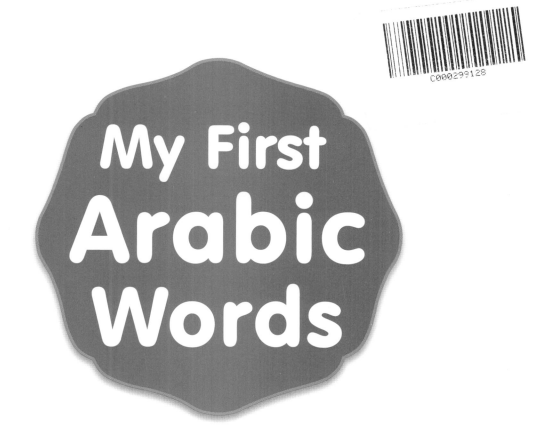

My First Arabic Words

Mohd. Harun Rashid
Mohammad Imran Erfani

Goodword

Project editor: Saniyasnain Khan
Edited by: Edward Kelzi
Art editor: Mateen Ahmad
Graphic design: K.K. Sahadevan, Slim Haokip
First published 2015
© Goodword Books 2015

Goodword Books
A-21, Sector 4, Noida-201301, India
Tel. +91-8588822672, +91120-4314871
email: info@goodwordbooks.com
www.goodwordbooks.com

Goodword Books, Chennai
324, Triplicane High Road,
Triplicane, Chennai-600005
Tel. +9144-4352-4599
Mob. +91-9790853944, 9600105558
email: chennaigoodword@gmail.com

Goodword Books, Hyderabad
Tel. 04023000131, Mob. 07032641415
email: hyd.goodword@gmail.com

Islamic Vision Ltd.
426-434 Coventry Road, Small Heath
Birmingham B10 0UG, U.K.
Tel. 121-773-0137, Fax: 121-766-8577
e-mail: info@ipci-iv.co.uk
www.islamicvision.co.uk

IB Publisher Inc.
81 Bloomingdale Rd, Hicksville, NY 11801, USA
Tel. 516-933-1000, Fax: 516-933-1200
Toll Free: 1-888-560-3222
email: info@ibpublisher.com
www.ibpublisher.com

Printed in India

How to Use this Book

My First Arabic Words is an appealing book for children who are just starting to learn Arabic. Colourful and amusing pictures help young children to learn their first Arabic words.

Arabic translation

Easy-to-understand Arabic translations are given to put words and pictures into context.

Arabic transliteration

Transliterations of some words are also provided to help the young learners how to say something in Arabic.

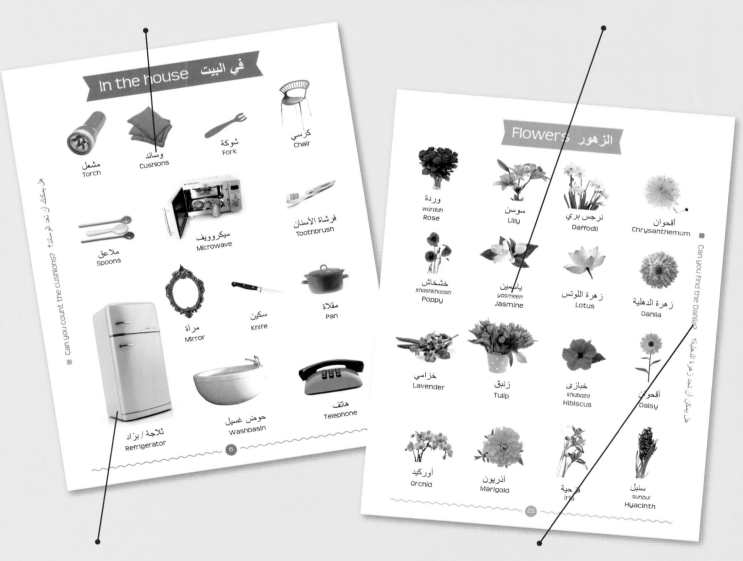

Pictures

Colourful and amusing pictures are used instead of illustrations to help young readers to identify the pictures and learn the words easily.

Questions

Each section has some questions for fun and a quick revision.

رأس
Head

شعر
Hair

أنف
Nose

عين
Eye

فم
Mouth

أذن
Ear

ذراع
Arm

ذقن
Chin

خد
Cheek

إصبع
Finger

يد
Hand

صدر
Chest

ركبة
Knee

رجل
Leg

قدم
Feet

● How many fingers do we have? كم إصبعاً لدينا؟

Can you find the handkerchief? هل تستطيع أن تعثر على المنديل؟

سترة / جاكيت
sutrah / jaket
Jacket

تي شيرت
T-Shirt

قميص
qamees
Shirt

قفازات
Gloves

وشاح
wishaah
Scarf

منديل
Handkerchief

جوارب
Socks

بلوفر / كنزة
Pullover

جينز
Jeans

بنطلون
Trousers

دنغري
Dungaree

قبعة
Hat

شباشب
Slippers

أحذية
ahdhiyah
Shoes

سراويل
Shorts

مشعل
Torch

وسائد
Cushions

شوكة
Fork

كرسي
Chair

ملاعق
Spoons

ميكروويف
Microwave

فرشاة الأسنان
Toothbrush

ثلاجة / برّاد
Refrigerator

مرآة
Mirror

سكين
Knife

مقلاة
Pan

حوض غسيل
Washbasin

هاتف
Telephone

هل يمكنك أن تعد الوسائد؟ Can you count the cushions?

6

تلفزيون
Television

مصباح
Lamp

ساعة
Clock

طاولة
Table

صابون
Soap

معجون الأسنان
Toothpaste

شباك
Window

غسالة
Washing Machine

برميل النفايات
Garbage Can

باب
Door

أريكة
Sofa

What time is it on the clock؟ ما هو الوقت في الساعة؟

هل يمكنك أن تجد الكعكة المحلاة؟ ● Can you find the doughnuts?

بيضة
baydah
Eggs

شوكولا
shokola
Chocolate

خبز
khubz
Breads

كعكة محلاة
Doughnuts

زبدة
zubdah
Butter

فطيرة مسطحة ومدورة
Muffin

قهوة
Coffee

رقاقات
Wafers

شاي
Tea

حليب / لبن
Milk

كاتشب
Ketchup

بيتزا
bitzaa
Pizza

عسل
Honey

كرويسانتس
croisaants
Croissants

برغر
Burger

جبن
Cheese

سكر
sukkar
Sugar

بطاطس مقلية
French Fries

فطيرة
Pancake

حساء
Soup

لبن زبادي
Yogurt

جوز
jawz
Nuts

سندويتش / شطيرة
Sandwits / shateerah
Sandwich

عصير
'aseer
Juice

● Where is the honey?   أين السل؟

هل يمكنك أن تجد الجزر؟ Can you find the carrot?

عنب
'inab
Grapes

كمثرى
Pear

فراولة
Strawberry

مانجو
Mango

جوافة
Guava

برتقال
burtaqaal
Orange

أناناس
Pineapples

موز
mauz
Banana

خوخ/درّاق
Peach

برقوق/خوخ
Plum

كرز
Cherry

تفاح
tuffaah
Apples

ليمون
laymoon
Lemon

فطر
Mushroom

فلفل حلو
Bell Pepper

بروكلي
Broccoli

طماطم
tamaatim
Tomato

كرنب ملفوف
Cabbage

شمندر
Beet

فلفل حار
filfil haarr
Chili pepper

ثوم
thoom
Garlic

بطاطس
Potato

فجل
Radish

فاصوليا
String beans

جزر
jazar
Carrot

قثاء / خيار
Cucumber

بازلاء
bazillaa'
Pea

لفت نبات
Turnips

سبانخ
asbaankh
Spinach

بصل
basal
Onions

باذنجان
Eggplant

قرنبيط
Cauliflower

ما هو لون العنب؟   What colour are the grapes?

ذيل
Tail

ثعلب
Fox

قرد
Monkey

دب
Bear

فرو
Fur

حمار وحشي
Zebra

حافر
haafir
Hoof

ذئب
dhi'b
Wolf

برنيق / فرس النهر
Hippopotamus

زرافة
Giraffe

خرطوم
Trunk

فيل
feel
Elephant

كم من حيوانات لها قرون؟

● How many animals have horns?

باندا
Panda

قشرة جلد
Scales

ثعبان
Snake

حوت
hoot
Whale

قرون
Antlers

أيل
ayyil
Deer

غوريلا
Gorilla

زعنفة
Fin

دلفين
Dolphin

بدة
Mane

خطم
Snout

حقيبة
Pouch

أسد
asad
Lion

تمساح
Crocodile

كنغر
Kangaroo

جمل
jamal
Camel

قرن
Horn

وحيد القرن
Rhinoceros

كفوف
Paws

نمر
Tiger

شبل
Cub (Lion)

جرو
Puppy (Dog)

حمل
Baby Lamb (Lamb)

فلو
filw
Foal (Horse)

قطيطة
Kitten (Cat)

فرخ / صوص
Chick (Hen)

Where is the kitten? أين القطيطة؟

صاعور
Kid (Goat)

جرو
Pup (Wolf)

فيل
Calf (Elephant)

عجل
'ijl
Calf (Cow)

بطيطة
Duckling (Duck)

شبل
Cub (Panda)

بوم
Owl

رفراف
Kingfisher

نحام
Flamingo

مخالب
Talons

نسر
Eagle

أبو منجل
Scarlet Ibis

يمامة
Dove

سلوى
salwa
Quail

منقار
Beak

غرنوق
Crane

Where is hoopoe?
أين الهدهد؟

ريشة
reeshah
Feather

طاووس
Peacock

نعامة
Ostrich

أجنحة
ajnihah
Wings

نورس
Seagull

ببغاء
Parrot

هدهد
hudhud
Hoopoe

غراب
ghurab
Crow

نقار الخشب
Woodpecker

إوز
Swan

بالونة
Balloon

سيارة
sayyaarah
Car

دراجة نارية
Motorcycle

هليكوبتر
Helicopter

سفينة
safeenah
Ship

حفارة
Excavator

طائرة
taa'irah
Aeroplane

قارب
Boat

ترام
taraam
Tram

قطار
qitaar
Train

صاروخ
Rocket

حافلة
haafilah
Bus

ما هو لون الترام؟

● What colour is the tram?

16

جندي
Soldier

طبيب
tabeeb
Doctor

طاه
taahin
Chef

طيار
Pilot

محام
Lawyer

ممرضة
Nurse

مهندس
Engineer

رجل إطفاء
Fire Fighter

نجار
Carpenter

خياط
Tailor

رائد الفضاء
Astronaut

ساعي البريد
saa'il bareed
Postman

حلاق
hallaq
Barber

معلم
mu'allim
Teacher

مدير
Manager

When do we visit the doctor? متى نذهب للطبيب؟

قمح
qamh
Wheat

ذرة
Corn

فزاعة
Scarecrow

جرارة
Tractor

بقرة
baqarah
Cow

حصان
hisaan
Horse

بط
Duck

ماعز
maa'iz
Goat

خروف
kharoof
Sheep

ديك
Rooster

● What colour is the tractor? ما هو لون الجرارة؟

حقل
Field

طاحونة هوائية
Wind mill

حصادة
Harvester

كوكيز بسكويت
Cookies

كاميرا
kaamira
Camera

أكواب ورقية
Paper Cups

نظام جهاز الموسيقى
Music System

هدايا
hadaaya
Present

مفرقعات نارية
Crackers

صفارة الميلاد
Birthday Whistle

قبعة
Hats

طاسات وملاعق
Bowls & Spoons

مشروبات غازية
Soft Drinks

شمعة
sham'ah
Candle

مناديل ورقية
Paper Napkins

حلوى
halwa
Candies

بالونات
Balloons

How many balloons are there? كم بالون هناك؟

صراف آلي
ATM Machine

إشارات المرور
Traffic Light

حافلة
haafilah
Bus

شرطة
shurtah
Police

ما هو لون الحافلة؟

What colour is the bus?

مسجد
masjid
Mosque

هيكل
Temple

كنيسة
Church

مدرسة
madrasah
School

فندق
Hotel

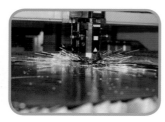

مصنع
Factory

مستشفى
mustashfa
Hospital

منتزه
muntazah
Park

محطة سكة الحديد
Railway Station

محل
mahall
Shop

مطار
Airport

مطعم
mat'am
Restaurant

غابة
Forest

جزيرة
jazeerah
Island

بحيرة
Lake

جبل
jabal
Mountains

ثلج
Snow

قمر
qamar
Moon

نجوم
nujoom
Stars

شلال
Waterfall

شمس
shams
Sun

نهر
River

مطر
Rain

صحراء
sahraa'
Desert

بحر
bahr
Sea

سحاب / غيمة
sahaab / ghaymah
Cloud

Which season follows spring? أيّ فصل يأتي بعد الربيع؟

طبخ
tabkh
Cooking

ألعاب فيديو
Videogame

تدوين / بلوغينغ
Blogging

حياكة / كروشيه
Crocheting

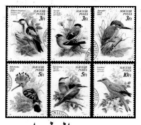

جمع الطوابع
Philately
(stamp collection)

جمع العملة
Numismatics
(coin collection)

كتابة إبداعية
Creative writing

حفظ الأسماك
Fish keeping

سحر
Magic

رقص
Dance

صنع المجوهرات
Jewelry making

حياكة
Knitting

آلات موسيقية
Musical instruments

رسم الألوان
Painting

غناء
Singing

رسوم كاريكاتورية
rusoom karikaturiyyah
Caricatures

ما هي هوايتك المفضلة؟

Which is your favorite hobby?

تزلج على الجليد
Ice Skating

رياضة بدنية / جمباز
Gymnastic

كرة القدم
Football

تنس/ كرة المضرب
Tennis

ركوب الدراجات
Cycling

كريكيت
Cricket

كرة السلة
Basketball

مصارعة
musaara'ah
Wrestling

كرة الطائرة
Volleyball

كرة الطاولة
Table Tennis

فنون عسكرية / قتاليّة
Martial Arts

ريشة
Badminton

بيسبول
Baseball

بلياردو
Billiards and pool

How many balls can you see on the pool table?

كم كرة يمكنك أن تراها على طاولة البلياردو؟

عشب
Grass

أرجوحة
urjoohah
See-saw

شجرة
shajarah
Tree

سنجاب
Squirrel

فراشة
faraashah
Butterfly

كلب
Dog

راكب الدراجة الهوائية
Cyclist

لوح التزلج
Skateboard

عربة أطفال
Pram

دكة
dikkah
Bench

أرجوحة
urjoohah
Swing

حلبة زالقة
Slide

هل يمكنك أن ترى السنجاب؟ ● Can you see the squirrel?

Flowers الزهور

 وردة
wardah
Rose

سوسن
Lilly

نرجس بري
Daffodil

أقحوان
Chrysanthemum

خشخاش
khashkhaash
Poppy

ياسمين
yasmeen
Jasmine

زهرة اللوتس
Lotus

زهرة الدهلية
Dahlia

خزامي
Lavender

زنبق
Tulip

خبازى
khubaza
Hibiscus

أقحوان
Daisy

أوركيد
Orchid

آذريون
Marigold

قزحية
Iris

سنبل
sunbul
Hyacinth

Can you find the Dahlia?

هل يمكنك أن تجد زهرة الدهلية؟

بانجو
Banjo

بيانو
bayaano
Piano

ساكسفون
Saxophone

بوق فرنسي
French horn

تشيلو
Cello

مزمار
mizmaar
Flute

دف تامبورين
duf tambureen
Tambourine

طبل
Drum

ميكروفون
mikrofon
Microphone

مكبرات الصوت
Speakers

بوق
Bugle

خشخاش
Bongos

غيتار
ghitaar
Guitar

كمان
kaman
Violin

ترومبون
Trombone

مزمار القربة
Bagpipes

كم من الآلة موسيقية لديها أوتار؟

How many instruments have strings?

الوقت Time

وقت الصباح
Morning Time

وقت تنظيف الأسنان
Toothbrush Time

وقت الفطور
waqtul futoor
Breakfast Time

وقت الغداء
Lunch Time

وقت العشاء
waqtul 'ashaa'
Dinner Time

وقت النوم
Bed Time

وقت الدراسة
Class Time

وقت الاستيقاظ
Wake-up Time

وقت المدرسة
waqtul madrasah
School Time

وقت رواية القصص
Story Time

وقت الليل
Night Time

وقت اللعب
Waqtul la'b
Play Time

When do you have dinner? متى تتعشى؟

نظيف
Clean

قذر
Dirty

كبير
kabeer
Big

صغير
sagheer
Small

جديد
jadeed
New

قديم
qadeem
Old

رطب
Wet

جاف
Dry

Can you see the shoes? هل يمكن أن ترى الأحذية؟

نحيل
Thin

سمين
Fat

سريع
saree'
Fast

بطيء
batee'
Slow

طويل
Long

قصير
Short

خشن
khashin
Rough

ناعم
naa'im
Smooth

خفيف
Light

ثقيل
Heavy

مغلق
mughlaq
Close

مفتوح
Open

مليء
mali'
Full

فارغ
faarigh
Empty

ناعم
Soft

صلب
Hard

ساخن
Hot

بارد
Cold

يسار
yasar
Left

يمين
yameen
Right

داخل
Inside

خارج
Outside

How many bottles are there?   كم زجاجة هناك؟

سبورة / لوح طبشور
Blackboard

فصل دراسي / صف
Classroom

كتاب
Book

قلم رصاص
qalamu rasas
Pencil

قلم
qalam
Pen

مقص
Scissors

دفتر / كراسة
Notebook

ممحاة
Eraser

مسطرة
mistarah
Ruler

هل هناك من أقلام تلوين؟

● How many crayons are there?

أقلام تلوين / كريون
Crayons

كرة أرضية
Globe

كمبيوتر
kambiwtar
Computer

صمغ لاصق
Samgh laasiq
Glue

مربع الغداء
Lunch Box

حقيبة مدرسية
School Bag

زي مدرسي
School Uniform

منضدة
mindadah
Desk

كرسي الشاطئ
kursiyyush shaati'
Beach chair

كابوريا / سلطعون
Crab

صدف
Seashell

دلو
Bucket

نظارة
Goggles

قبعة
Hat

قناع الغوص
Diving mask

مجرفة
Shovel

سفينة
safeenah
Ship

حرس /منقذ بحري
Lifeguard

حقيبة
Bag

كرة
kurah
Ball

منارة
manaarah
Light House

قصر الرمال
qasrur rimaal
Sand Castle

لوح التزلج
Surfboard

● Where is the ball? أين الكرة؟

أخضر (أوراق)
Green

أحمر (صندوق البريد)
ahmar
Red

أزرق (جينز)
azraq
Blue

وردي (ديزي)
Pink

أرجواني (فراشة)
Purple

برتقالي (جزر)
Orange

أسود (الغراب)
aswad
Black

أصفر (دوار الشمس)
asfar
Yellow

مربع (لوحة كاروم)
murabba'
Square

بيضوي (مرآة)
Oval

دائرة (ساعة)
Daa'irah
Circle

مخروط (ايس كريم)
Cone

مستطيل (سبورة)
Rectangle

هرم
haram
Pyramid

نجم (نجم البحر)
najm
Star

هلال (القمر)
hilaal
Crescent

هل يمكنك أن تجد الغراب؟ ● Can you find the crow?